Empowerment Selling

STOP Selling and START Fulfilling Your Customers' Needs

by
Mark Bornstein
Fran Fisher

Dear Ann Marie,

connect!

clarify!

cultivate!

♡ Fran Fisher
5-17-14

Front Cover Artist: Vanaigraphics
Editor: Linda L. Lane

ISBN 13: 978-0-9798754-1-0

Library of Congress Number: 2014901636

Manufactured, typeset, and printed in the United States of America.

Table of Contents

Empowerment Selling
STOP Selling and START Fulfilling Your Customers' Needs

Introduction

It is literally true that you can succeed best and quickest by helping others to succeed. Napoleon Hill

As the Internet evolves and technological advances continue—along with dramatic changes in the business economy——consumers are now better informed and have access to a vast amount of quality information , that enables them to be more knowledgeable about products and services. As a result, selling to this "new" customer requires a new approach. Many people in the selling game are realizing that their former sales methods are no longer effective.

Empowerment Selling

Galileo said: *We cannot teach people anything; we can only help them discover it within themselves.* This philosophy is key to the shift in sales that is now required.

Successful professional athletes, executives, and entertainers work with a coach. Coaching is an empowering paradigm. It is not about telling the client who or how to "be" or how to do their life or work. Rather, it is about helping them bring forth the highest and best that is within them.

Empowerment Selling demonstrates the paradigm shift from selling a product or service by having to convince the customer that it's the best product/service (which, at the extreme, would be high pressure sales) to facilitating the customer in a client-generated solution for a successful outcome which helps build collaborative, ongoing relationships—and a long-term sales win/win strategy.

We are presenting a powerful approach we call *The 3C Principle:* Connect. Clarify. Cultivate. The 3C Principle focuses on the essence of this underlying empowerment philosophy for effective sales versus detailed mechanics or formulated scripts and the inference that the seller knows more than the customer.

This principle of empowerment is recognized by the International Coach Federation (ICF), an international association for coaches. Personal Professional Coaching is based on a key assumption that everyone is fundamentally creative, capable, and resourceful. Within this foundation, the coach's responsibility is to:

- Discover, clarify, and align with what the client wants to achieve
- Encourage client self-discovery
- Elicit client-generated solutions and strategies
- Hold the client responsible and accountable

As you read Dana's story, we invite you to explore how your own life or your work could benefit by applying these principles. If you work with people, these principles are transferrable!

Empowerment Selling Inquiry: *How do I stop selling and start fulfilling my customers' needs?*

Mark Bornstein
Fran Fisher

February 2014

Note: We use the terms "customer" and "client" interchangeably to illustrate the global application of these principles in the market place.

Introducing Dana

Hi, I'm Dana. I have been working as a sales representative with Innovative Products for ten years. Life changed dramatically with my recent divorce and the responsibility of raising my 12 year-old son Brandon as a single parent. In addition to the challenges in my personal life, I find that my work life isn't as easy and profitable as in the past.

It is increasingly difficult for me to keep up with the transformations in our company culture, ongoing changes in technology, and trying to keep up with my clients' constantly changing needs in this stressful economic environment.

Selling has always been easy for me, and I enjoy the friendships I have built with my clients. However, the harder I work to fulfill my sales quotas, the less quality time I have to spend with my son, and my success as the he top sales executive in our company is eroding. I'm learning that being a friend and a product expert is not enough anymore.

Recently I had to face the fact that I was in jeopardy of losing my job if I didn't increase my sales performance. And, I had to acknowledge that my stress was affecting my sales performance, as well as my health and my relationship with my son. Fear became my motivator for learning what I needed to do to adapt in the face of all these changes.

Fortunately, I learned a fresh approach that has positively changed my life and work and, by extension, my personal life as well. It's called The 3 C Principle. These principles have provided the framework for my breakthrough to a whole new level of personal and professional success. And, I want to share them with you.

Chapter ONE

Is that the alarm? I could use more sleep… I already have a knot in my stomach… I know for sure there's no award for me today. What is happening to me?

As I pack Brandon's lunch with his favorite tuna sandwich, chips, apple, and oatmeal cookie, I help him get ready for school. I catch myself thinking about today's sales meeting, imagining the worst and dreading the inevitable disclosure that I've had another poor sales month. After almost ten award-winning years with the firm, my sales have slacked off dramatically. I feel queasy as I bolt down my cold dry toast and lukewarm coffee.

I am not very happy with myself today. I glance in the hall mirror on the way out the door, just long enough to check the hem of my gray pencil skirt and adjust my white cotton shirt collar over the collar of my navy blue blazer. I'm skipping the floral scarf I usually wear with this outfit. I don't have the time or patience to fuss with it this morning.

I continue the rushed routine of my morning as I drop off Brandon at his school, slowing down just long enough to give him a quick hug and a kiss. "Oh Mom," he protests, as he barely tolerates my display of affection. I manage to navigate through the line of noisy school busses and head for the Interstate for my 20-minute commute. Pulling into the office parking lot, I feel anxious and reluctant about going into the meeting. Taking a moment to collect myself, I drop off my purse and briefcase at my desk, quickly check messages, and grab a yellow note pad and pen. As I walk into the conference room, my colleagues are already there, waiting for the quarterly sales meeting to start. The hum of small talk is not loud enough to distinguish anything specific being said. I can already feel the room closing in on me.

Finally, Don Cummings, our regional Vice President comes in. He is a heavy-set man, bald, late 40s, and dressed in his usual khaki slacks and sports shirt. *Interesting, as low key as this company is, he expects us to call him "Mr. Cummings," not Don. We call all the other VPs by their first names.* After some brief chit chat, he begins the meeting.

I'm in a mental fog as he announces the sales awards for the quarter, my name is not mentioned—*no surprise!* I am happy for those who win but totally devastated that my numbers are so low. Embarrassed and depressed, my congratulations are halfhearted. I make my way toward the coffee and pastries at the back of the room, but the sweet smell of maple bars doesn't appeal to my nervous stomach.

Mr. Cummings calls out my name from across the room and gestures, indicating he wants me to meet with him in his office immediately. I enter his office, and he closes the door behind me. His office has no windows and it feels confining and stuffy. His desk is covered with piles of papers and file folders. He gestures for me to take the chair across from his desk and, without any niceties, proceeds to tell me that my sales performance is substandard, as if I didn't already know that.

"Dana, I don't understand what has happened to you. You're sales volume has dropped 25% and on top of that you've just lost a key company account. Rumor is that you were the problem. Furthermore, it appears from your sales reports that you are not getting into enough prospects' offices these days, and your sales conversion rate is below anybody else in the company—half what it used to be. "

I feel defensive. "Mr. Cummings, I know I lost that key account, but Franklin Supply Company had a better pricing structure, and they were willing to provide more services. I realize my numbers are down, and I know that I have to increase them. But, in my defense, this is the first time in ten years of success, I'm having a string of bad luck. I've always been able to out-perform the competition and to provide excellent service for our clients." I wipe my sweating hands on my skirt.

I feel panic rise as I realize that this isn't just a discussion of what I can do to improve—I could lose my job.

"I believe in the quality of our product and the mission of our company. I can't afford to have my income continue to drop, so I'm motivated both personally and professionally. Please give me a chance to turn this around."

"Dana, if it wasn't for your excellent track record with this company, I would be forced to let you go. But you've been a loyal employee and everybody is entitled to one bad streak. However, this downward trend can't continue. I'll give you six months to improve your sales. I suggest you make sure all of your customers are happy. And, let me know how I can best support you. We don't want to lose you."

"Mr. Cummings, thank you. I will get to work and turn this around, I promise. Thank you."

My head is pounding, my stomach is in knots, and I can barely hold myself together as I dash for the women's restroom. Hiding in the first stall, I let the dam burst as silently as I can contain myself. I hear another toilet flush, so I know someone else is in the restroom.

I'm a single mom. I need this job, and I've never felt so scared and humiliated in my life. I know my numbers have dropped, and I just can't figure out what I am doing wrong. I guess I'll have to work harder, but I don't know what to do differently.

Clients are more knowledgeable and price savvy today, with the advent of the Internet. They do their own research and do their own product and pricing comparisons on line. I really wish we were more competitive with some of our products. It seems like we are losing our competitive edge. I'm just not finding the right products to fulfill the needs of my clients. Boy, it was easier when I started ten years ago. Or maybe it was my willingness to try anything to make a sale. Or, just maybe it was the fact that we had a sales manager in those days.

It was really helpful having a sales manager holding me accountable and helping me strategize how to best work with my accounts. That was another change that was made as a result of margins tightening! I really can't deal with this right now. I really have to get out of here. I don't want anyone to see me in this condition.

I collect myself as best I can, go straight to my office, pick up my briefcase and purse, and head over to the ball field to pick up Brandon at soccer practice. This has been his favorite sport. He started playing two years ago when he turned 10. I covered the passenger seat with a bath towel on soccer days. Brandon, grass stained and muddy, climbs into the car.

I ask him about his day at school. He answers me, but I don't hear a word he is saying.

"Brandon, please take a shower and work on your homework while I fix dinner."

"OK. What's for dinner?"

"I don't know, honey. Please don't bother me right now."

He is such a good kid. I am really not being very fair to him right now.

I feel alone. I need to talk to someone, preferably an adult. After starting a pot of boiling water for the macaroni, I decide to call Carol.

"Carol, it's Dana."

"Hi, Dana, how are you?"

"Horrible. I really need a friendly shoulder tonight. Can you come over after dinner?"

"Sure, what's wrong?"

"Work. I'll tell you when you get here."

Still feeling shaky and somewhat out of control, I put the macaroni in the boiling water and pour myself a glass of red wine. As I sip on the wine, I'm thinking about my conversation with Mr. Cummings.

He's not being fair. I've given too much to this company and worked too hard for him to talk to me like that.

I call up the stairs, "Brandon, dinner is ready."

In a few minutes, he is bounding down the stairs two at a time. In the kitchen, he notices my mood.

"Mom, what's wrong?"

"I had a really bad day at work today, honey. My boss is very unhappy with my sales, so I really need to work harder for the next few months, and I'm going to need your help."

"What kind of help?" he asks reluctantly.

"Oh, I don't even know yet. I may have to work longer hours for a while, but I really don't know yet."

"Oh, *man!*" he groans.

After dinner, Carol arrives with her usual flamboyant flourish and flair that matches her big hair, home-dyed red, and those colorful gypsy outfits she always wears. She sweeps up Brandon with a big bear hug, "How's my favorite soccer player?" she asks, and then turns her attention to me.

"Ok, Dana, what's going on?"

Brandon escapes to his bedroom.

"First, a glass of wine."

Pouring the wine, I tell Carol, "I was called on the carpet today for having a big decrease in sales.

After the meeting, Mr. Cummings called me into his office and warned me that I'll lose my job if I don't improve. I've lost a big account, and he said that I am not seeing enough prospects. You know, Carol, I've busted my bustle for the last ten years. I don't deserve to be treated that way. Then on top of it, he tells me that I have to participate in the company's golf tournament next month. I don't have clubs, bag, shoes, or clothing for golfing. I'm not even interested in playing golf."

"Didn't you play golf in college?"

"I did, but that was long time ago. I was never really that good."

"Can't you get out of it?"

"I'm treading on thin ice right now. I can't afford to not show up and be a good sport for the annual company tournament."

"Dana, why don't you go to Par's Golf Course and Pro Shop, check out lessons, and get a new set of clubs. You know, Dana, you'll probably have fun, and it will get you out of your routine. Maybe you'll even meet someone."

"Nice thought, but right now I can't even think of that."

2:05 AM. It helped talking to Carol--lightened me up a bit in the moment. But, here I am in the middle of the night, and my head is spinning with worry and questions: How am I going to increase my sales? What in the world am I going to do?

2:06 AM. Wide awake, my clock clicks every time it flips to the next minute.

Chapter TWO

After a restless night worrying, I realize I need to find out what is preventing me from making sales. After I get Brandon off to school, I'll call my contact at the account that I lost to Franklin and see if they'll give me feedback on why I lost the account. Mr. Cummings said that *I* was the problem. I can't face them right now, though. I think I'll call Charlie, my favorite client first—talking with him will bolster my confidence.

"Wonderful, Charlie. Thanks. I'll be at your office in an hour."

Charlie has been a loyal client in the past, and before that he and my dad were close friends. When I was younger, Charlie was a frequent guest at our family holiday dinners. How will I ask him to give me honest feedback on me as his sales rep? Will he be honest with me? I hope he can help me see something that I need to learn, but I also don't want to jeopardize our relationship.

"Hi, I'm Dana, and I have an appointment with Charlie."

As I wait in the reception area, I hear the hum of a copier and a phone ringing down a hall.

A friendly, efficient receptionist gestures for me to go right in. She's new. I don't recognize her.

As I walk back to Charlie's office, I feel the butterflies in my stomach. Charlie waves me in with a big smile on his weathered face and his dark brown eyes always make me feel warmly welcomed. As he gets up from behind his desk and extends his handshake, he asks, "Hi Dana, what's up?" Charlie, a medium built man with a full head of neatly combed white hair, is probably in his early sixties and nowhere near thinking about retiring. I smell that familiar aroma of his pipe smoke on his wool tweed sports jacket, even though he doesn't smoke in his office. It always reminds me of my dad. I think my dad must have smoked the same brand of cherry-flavored pipe tobacco.

"Charlie, thank you for meeting me on such short notice."

As soon as I am seated I say, "As a good friend and a former customer, I'd like to ask you a very serious personal question."

"Of course, what is it, Dana?"

"Charlie, my sales have fallen off over the last year, and Mr. Cummings, my VP, made it very clear yesterday that if I don't improve my sales in the next six months, I'll be looking for a new job. I really can't afford to do that. I have ten years invested in this company and a son to support. After a sleepless night, I have come to the conclusion that I need to assess my sales skills, and I am hoping that you will provide me with honest feedback. I promise I will not get upset. Anything you say, I will truly value, because I have a lot of respect for you."

"Do you really want to hear the truth?"

All of a sudden, I am aware that I am tightly gripping the smooth wooden arms of the chair. I flash on how tense I am when I am in the dentist chair. I make an effort to take a deep breath, let my shoulders down, and relax my hands.

"Yes, Charlie, I do. The truth is very important to me. Don't hold back."

"OK, then. Here goes. Over the years I have known you as a sales rep, you used to provide excellent customer service. You went above and beyond on many occasions. I enjoyed working with you because of our friendship. However, you know that I make the purchasing decisions here, and I work with numerous other vendors. So, I really feel that I have a sense of what a sales representative should be offering to me as the client.

"One of the things I became disappointed with was that you didn't take the time to determine my company's needs. Our needs have changed in the last few years. Besides not asking, you haven't been listening when I've told you what I wanted. Instead, you were attempting to sell your products without concern for our real needs. Other vendors take the time to ask how we are going to use a product, what it's going to replace, is there a better way of doing it, or what we want to achieve. Or, perhaps we need to customize something. They show a sincere interest in our company and its success.

When I found something wrong with your product —when it didn't fit our specific needs—you tried to minimize my objections rather than respecting them and learning what it would take to meet our requirements."

"Oh, my gosh, Charlie, you are absolutely right. I didn't realize what I was doing! I am so sorry! Is there anything else?"

Charlie goes to a small cooler near his desk, pulls out two bottles of cold water, and offers me one. I welcomed the breather. He takes a drink and then says, "Yes, one more thing, Dana, since you asked. In the last few years, I feel that you came here only when you needed to make a sale. In the past, you were successful because your company didn't have the competition it does now, and we needed your product. But our needs have changed and so has the market."

Swallowing hard, "Charlie, thank you for being so honest. I can see this has been hard for you, but I really appreciate your kindness in telling me the truth. I see where I have taken you for granted as a client due to the friendship we developed over the years, and I have not been cognizant of your company's needs. I wonder if I am doing that to other clients as well. You are being a true friend by telling me how you feel and how my behavior has impacted my serving you as a valued client.

"Charlie, would you be willing to meet with me for lunch in a week or two, so we can further discuss

27

your feedback? I clearly need some time to digest all this. Your friendship and your business are very important to me. I want the opportunity to really understand your company's changing needs."

"Of course, Dana. Give yourself some time. Call me when you are ready."

On the way home, I hug the steering wheel and let my tears flow. Whew, that was brutal. I thought all this time I was doing a great job. I'm so embarrassed. I plug in my favorite Whitney Houston CD to drown my thoughts. I know I will process all this this evening, but I need an emotional break right now.

I have a few minutes before time to pick up Brandon. I grab some note paper, clear a spot on my kitchen desk, take a deep breath, and jot down some thoughts while they are still fresh in my mind. Charlie just gave me some really valuable feedback:

- I have not been listening.

- I am telling versus asking questions.
- I minimize objections versus respecting them.
- I am asking the wrong questions.
- I am perceived as needy/have to make the sale.
- I am doing product information dumps.
- I am running my agenda versus supporting the client's agenda.
- I am taking clients for granted.

Across the bottom of the pad, I write: *I will discover what it takes to be successful in these changing times.* On a separate scrap of paper I write "TO DO TONIGHT:"

(1) Par's Golf Course and Pro Shop

(2) Brandon to the library

(3) Look for current books on selling

Chapter THREE

"Brandon, I promised to take you to the library tonight, didn't I? Well, we're going to stop at Par's Golf Course and Pro Shop on the way home and then go to the library after dinner, OK?"

I really can't afford to make this expense. I guess I'll just have to put it on the credit card. Company golf tournaments are such a waste of time, but I have no choice. I'll go and participate...what a bore.

The weather forecasts rain for this evening, and as I look at the sky, those dark gray clouds are reflecting my heavy mood. I dread the prospect of having to make decisions tonight on things I don't feel I can afford. And Brandon will probably nag at me to buy him something.

Pulling up to the golf shop, Brandon asks me, "What are you getting, Mom?

"I need to get a set of golf clubs and shoes for the company golf tournament."

"Cool, can I get something?"

"We'll see," I say, painfully aware this is what I say when I really want to say "no."

Umbrella in hand and navigating around puddles in the parking lot, I take a few deep breaths of the air. I have to admit that fresh fragrance of this clean air is lifting my spirits. Entering Par's, I am already overwhelmed with how big the store is. I really don't know where to start to look for what I need.

After browsing for several minutes, a tall, athletic-looking brunette woman approaches me. She is dressed in smart crisp golf attire in color-coordinated shades of olive green that look stunning next to her tanned skin. She looks like someone who spends a great deal of time outdoors. I notice her Par's Golf Shop name badge says "MaryAnn."

"Hello, I'm MaryAnn, one of the golf pros here at Par's. What are your needs today?"

"I'm really not much of a golfer, but I have to participate in my company's tournament next month. I have no clubs, shoes, or proper golf attire."

"Before I show you anything, why don't we sit and talk? Would you care for something to drink?"

"Yes, that would be very nice, thanks. My name is Dana." I am already feeling quite comfortable with this woman.

MaryAnn asks me an unusual question, "What is most important for you in preparing for this event?"

"I really can't afford to purchase clubs, bag, shoes, and clothing for the event, but it's critical for me to show up and participate. I need to show the boss I am a team player and create a positive image for our company."

"OK. You said you are really not a golfer. What does that mean? Have you ever played before?"

"Yes, I played in college, but that was a long time ago. I haven't picked up a club since then. In fact, I'd do anything to get out of it, but I'm feeling tremendous pressure from my boss."

"What do you want, then?"

"To play and not make a fool out of myself!" I throw my hands in the air and laugh at myself. MaryAnn smiles.

"Dana, here's a club. Please swing it for me."

Holding the club, I take a swing. I notice the smell of leather coming from the glove rack next to where we are standing.

"How did that feel?"

"Awkward, uncomfortable, clumsy. I told you I'm not very good."

"May I refresh your memory on how to hold a golf club?

"Sure!"

"Now take a swing. How does that feel?"

"Much more comfortable."

Out of the corner of my eye, I see Brandon looking at golf clubs and he is talking with a sales associate. Oh, dear me...

"Great! And, by the way, you have a nice swing. May I make a suggestion regarding your stance?"

"Of course!"

"OK, stand like this, swing again, and notice how that feels."

"Boy, this is all coming back to me now. This actually feels pretty good."

"Dana, how much money do you want to spend?"

"Not much. I really can't afford it, but I will do what I need to do to make the appearance. Thank goodness for credit cards."

"Is it absolutely necessary that you purchase?"

"Do I have a choice?"

"Well, if you were to buy the bag, clubs, shoes and clothing, it would cost at least $800.00. However, if you rent the clubs and shoes, it's only $50."

"Really? I can rent everything?"

"Everything but the clothes."

"Also, we also offer brush-up lessons for people like you. We have a series of group lessons for $75 and private lessons for $150 each."

I can't believe the solution is so easy.

"MaryAnn, that's wonderful. When does the group lesson start?"

Brandon has disappeared out of my sight and now he is back, as if on cue. He doesn't hesitate to ask, "How about me, too, Mom?"

"I really can't afford that right now, Brandon. And, I don't have the time to drive you to golf lessons too, on top of everything else I have going on right now."

I wish I could be more there for him right now.

As we are walking out the double doors, Mary Ann comes rushing out the door with my umbrella in hand. I enjoy another deep breath of the fresh rain air before getting into the car.

Driving home, I feel good about my experience with MaryAnn. Why didn't she sell me anything? She listened. She asked me questions. And, instead of selling me a new set of clubs, she offered me the option of renting them. She did everything so differently than I would have done. I'm sure she works on commission. Why didn't she sell me the $800 package? What happened?

I really like MaryAnn. I felt like she really cared about me. Maybe Charlie was right. MaryAnn put my needs first.

I want to spend more time with MaryAnn. I think I could learn from her and not just about golf.

Chapter FOUR

As I drive to my first group lesson with MaryAnn, I feel as excited as I did when I was nine years old and I got to ride a horse for the first time. The memory of that feeling is so strong it brings back the smell of fresh hay and the warmth of the sunshine on my face that day.

I can't wait to ask MaryAnn some questions about our first encounter.

MaryAnn greets me as I walk in. "Hi, Dana, are you ready for your first lesson?" She is wearing another fashionable golf outfit today. This time, it's a warm golden-colored golf shirt that goes great with her brown eyes and beige slacks.

In the background I hear the whack of clubs connecting with balls over at the driving range.

"Sure, but before the class starts, may I ask you a question?"

"Of course."

"I'm puzzled. When I came into the shop last week to buy golf clubs, shoes, and clothes, you didn't even try to sell it to me. Instead, you offered me the option of renting, which really works much better for me."

With a smile, she said, "I too had problems with sales until I met a very smart individual who mentored me, showed me a fresh approach, and taught me how to help people make a buying decision. It's made all the difference in my success, and now I enjoy what I am doing so much more."

"Is this an approach you can share with me?"

"Yes, and I will be happy to spend a few minutes with you today after your lesson." We head over to the class, our shoe cleats crunching on the concrete until we step onto the grass.

After the lesson, MaryAnn and I sat for a few minutes, talking. "Thank you. That was a great lesson. I feel more confident with my swing already."

"Great, let's have some coffee. I promised I would share with you my secret to sales success. It is called the 3C Principle." With that, MaryAnn pulls out a well-worn bright yellow laminated card and explains that it was given to her by her mentor several years ago. "My mentor explained to me that this principle is based on empowerment. He showed me *Webster's Dictionary* where is says that 'empowerment is the ability to give power or authority'. So, in the case of a sales transaction, this is me granting the power or authority to the customer or potential customer. Today I will share the first C, which stands for Connect."

"Connect, what do you mean by Connect?"

"Remember when you came in last week, and I took the time to ask questions and learn about you and your needs?"

"Yes, I remember that it felt strange to me that you didn't take me to the golf clubs right away."

"It was more important for me to first build trust with you. To build trust requires giving up what I want and focusing on what you want. What did I do with you that gave you a sense of trust or comfort with me?"

"Your greeting was warm, personable, and you were sincerely interested in me and my needs. You asked me questions that helped me discover what my needs really were. And, when you gave me the option to rent, you solved my financial problem."

MaryAnn is smiling. "Dana, you are very observant. That's right. Did you also notice that the sale wasn't important to me? What was most important was finding out what was right for you."

"That's what confused me so much."

"I was confused too when I first learned the 3C Principle because my natural inclination was to sell my product to the customer. It was hard work. I began to realize it was not satisfying, fulfilling, or productive. That was when I met my mentor. What he taught seemed counter intuitive at the time. But I tried it, and I was amazed at the difference it made in my results."

"Please tell me more. I suspect I need to learn this lesson."

"Connect" is all about relationship. You will achieve greater sales results in the long run and obtain personal satisfaction when you change your focus to understanding the client's needs rather than needing to make the sale.

"Taking the time to ask the questions that reveal the client's needs, values, and desires will make it much easier to understand and then fulfill their needs and wants."

"How do you do that?"

"Remember when you came in last week? I asked you numerous questions, none of which dealt with golf clubs. What I learned from you is that the golf clubs weren't important, but what was important was your need to be present at the tournament and gain favor from your boss. The fact is that you are not committed to being a golfer. If I had sold you the clubs, you would have eventually felt resentful, unsatisfied with a set of clubs you'd bought, and you'd have left with a bad taste toward me and my company. However, by fulfilling what you really need, you have a good feeling about me and my company. There is a much greater possibility that you will come back some day or refer your friends. Bottom line, Dana, you may even enjoy taking up golf again."

"Wow, I see what you mean. Please tell me more."

"Here are some guidelines that I learned from my mentor."

3C Principle

First C - Connect

- Be service oriented versus sales focused
- Be caring and fully present; LISTEN deeply
- Be considerate of the client's agenda, not your own
- Be a collaborative partner
- Be committed to the quality of the relationship

"This sounds very intriguing. I want to try this. How do I start?"

"Describe to me your typical sales call."

"I go in and show our new products and ask for the sale."

"This week, ask your prospects, 'What is the one thing I can help you with today?' and then listen."

"It's that easy?"

"Once you show care and ask questions that will benefit your prospective customer, it becomes that easy. You will have to shift your priorities from making the sale to doing what is in the best interest for the buyer. That's the empowerment approach. That will be your higher purpose.

"This week, if you really want to try this, focus on leaving your prospect with these bottom line messages:

- I care about you.
- What is the one thing that I can help you with today?
- Our relationship is more important to me than the sale."

"Thank you, I am going to give this a try. What about the other Cs?"

"Once you feel comfortable with the first connecting and building relationship, give me a call, and I'll be happy to share the Second C with you. In the meantime, practice your golf swing!!"

The phone is ringing as I walk in the door. I see on the caller ID that it's Carol, so I pull up a kitchen chair and sit down to answer her call. "Hi Carol! I am so glad you called."

"Dana, how is it going?"

"Well, right now, Carol, I am overwhelmed with realizations of how I got off track and how much I have to learn to keep up with changing times! Do you have a few minutes while I vent?"

"Sure, that's what I called for—to check in on you."

"Thanks. OK, for one thing, I completely forgot some of the fundamentals, especially the one about building trust in the relationship with my clients. Over time, when sales got harder to make, my objective became more about making a sale and less on building connection in the customer relationship. I realize too that I got complacent—downright lazy at times—when sales were easier to close. I also see that the stress in my personal life really knocked me off the rails way more than I realized. The good news is that I met a woman this week at Par's who is not only refreshing me on the fundamentals of sales, she is showing me a new approach that really resonates for me. I can't wait to try out what I am learning from her.

"Having said that, I am also feeling some resistance to changing what I am doing. Ugh...I did appreciate her point, though. She said that even golf pros have to change their game every time new technology improves the golf club."

"You will be OK, girlfriend! And remember, I am here for you, anytime."

Chapter FIVE

3:14 AM…tick…3:15… tick… I can't sleep again tonight, thinking about my conversation with MaryAnn. Building relationships based on caring and questioning. It seems so simple. I have three new prospects I am meeting with tomorrow, and I really need the sales. I don't want to do what I have done in the past, because it hasn't been working. I am going to try this new approach and see if it creates different results for me. I certainly hope MaryAnn is right.

Tuesday
Whew, I did it!! It felt different today. I feel good. No one said, 'no,' and no one got upset with me. In fact, all three invited me back to present a proposal. I'm amazed at how far I got by just asking questions and listening.

A couple of times I caught myself trying to push product, but it didn't seem to work. So, I reverted back to what was important to the client instead.

I also had the opportunity to get to know more about these people on a personal basis.

I actually think Mr. McGregor was pleased that I was taking the time to learn about his company's needs. I never did that before. The fact is, I noticed that the less I talked about my products, the more I built rapport with him.

I feel so good about my experience today, trying this new approach. I am going to reward myself for my courage and commitment to turn things around. I know! I'll buy myself a bouquet of pink carnations. The fragrance will fill the house, and they always last a long time, too.

I roll over, feeling my sore shoulder and arm muscles from practicing my golf swing.

I can hardly wait until tomorrow to try this again. I know now what MaryAnn meant when she said that this way of selling is more rewarding. I actually enjoyed myself today. I definitely felt less anxious once I began to build a connection.

I have two more appointments tomorrow. Tomorrow, I will concentrate more on fact finding in order to gain clarity about their needs.

Friday

This has been the best week I've had in years. I feel more energized. I am discovering a sincere desire to help my customers. Focusing on their needs gives me a different attitude and feeling to the whole experience. I don't think they looked at me as just a sales person, but rather as someone trying to help.

Whether or not I even make the sale isn't as important because I know they trust me and respect my opinion and that will reflect favorably on my company. I am beginning to believe that this new approach is going to provide me with the tools to help me turn things around. I certainly hope so. I have a mortgage payment due very soon.

I used to depend on my sales manager to hold me accountable. Now I realize I want to hold myself accountable. I don't exactly know how yet, but I want to learn.

I hear the digital noises of Brandon's video game. I call up the stairs, "Come on, Brandon, we are going to dinner and a movie tonight. It's been a good week, and I have a surprise for you."

Video game noise stops. I hear shoes dropping to the floor and something else too. I have no idea what, but my guess it's something falling out of his closet. Here he comes. I didn't have to ask twice.

"Mom, what's the surprise? "

"I've made arrangements for you to take golf lessons with me, and I want to thank you for being patient with me. I know I haven't been much fun the past several months."

Chapter SIX

Monday

3 PM. I just finished my last appointment. Whew! That went well. Better than I expected. Now I am excited about seeing MaryAnn for my second group lesson and to share with her how good I am feeling about the First C Principle: "Connect."

Brandon is at soccer practice until 5 PM, so I am free now for my next group lesson. I arrive ten minutes early, hoping to have a few words with Mary Ann privately before the lesson starts. As I approach the putting green, I take in the blue sky, fluffy white cumulous clouds lining the horizon, and the vibrant green of the freshly mowed grass.

Mary Ann is already there. She greets me as I approach. "Hi Dana! Are you ready for your lesson?"

"I can hardly wait!"

MaryAnn: "Tell me about your *connecting* this week. How did it go?"

I feel just like I did once in the third grade. It was our first day back from spring break, and I was bursting to share with my teacher that I had overcome my fear of horses and learned to ride.

"It worked *great, Mary Ann*. Last week I asked each of my new prospects, 'What is the one thing I can help you with today?' Not only did they tell me, but they allowed me the opportunity to learn more about their company and their products and their needs for the coming year. Instead of trying to sell them anything, I took notes and asked more questions. No one said 'no' to me. In fact, I am preparing proposals for each of them."

Others are gathering for the class now, so we start walking out to the putting green. What a gorgeous day! I feel lighthearted and hopeful for the first time in a very long time.

After the class, I linger with Mary Ann hoping for more time to discuss the Second C Principle.

"Dana, your swing is improving and your concentration on hitting the ball is excellent. How is it feeling for you?" Mary Ann is obviously still in golf instructor mode.

"You know, I think I could learn to enjoy playing golf again. Having instruction from you has given me new skills and more confidence with my golf game. Do you have a few minutes to talk about the next C? I'll buy coffee."

"I'll gladly take you up on your offer. It's a pleasure to share what I learned with someone who is committed to improvement."

We each pour our mug of coffee and stir in cream and sugar from the coffee bar available for customers. MaryAnn motions toward a comfortable seating area in one corner of the store. The sofas and chairs face large picture windows, so customers can enjoy the golf course in all its beauty. We get comfortable for our conversation.

MaryAnn remarks, "I think you learned the First C Principle lesson well."

"Thanks." Eagerly, I ask, "Now that I understand the First C 'Connect', what it the next C?"

"The Second C is *'Clarify'*. Having established connection, *clarifying* is facilitating the client in achieving clarity from their own authority. In other words, it's the opposite of manipulation. Your job is to support the client in discovering and choosing what they know is best for them.

"Remember when you came in for the golf clubs? The clarifying happened when I asked you questions to clarify what it was that you really wanted. In your case, it wasn't a set of new clubs, but rather how you were going to satisfy your boss."

"You also heard me and trusted me when I said I couldn't afford an $800 package."

"Dana, take out your notebook. I am going to give you a list of key elements of the Second C, 'Clarify'."

- Support the client in identifying what is best for them, from their point of view
- Assist the client in clearing the barriers to getting what they need
- Explore options and generate possibilities
- Empower the client's decision-making process
- Acknowledge and respect their choices

"So I think I am beginning to understand that we are to believe that the client actually knows what is best for them. But the part I am most stumped about is how do I help them gain the clarity?"

"Dana, it is all about control. Well, giving up the need to control, I mean. When you give up the need to control and place control with the customer, they trust you and the process, and that trust eliminates the fear of manipulation, and resistance to being 'sold to.' Now, you and your customer have the freedom to explore and expand possibilities, options, and alternatives. And, given that you both have an understanding about what they truly want; you can help them clear the barriers to having it."

Mary Ann sets her mug on the coffee table and leans toward me. I tune out the music playing through the store's speakers overhead and sharpen my focus for listening.

"In the past, we called that 'handling objections.' In the 3C Principle, we call it 'clearing what is in the way.' In the outdated model, it was my agenda to sell them on the product. In the 3C Principle—the empowerment approach—it is about supporting the client in having what they want—which is the best decision for them."

My attention is distracted just now. I am noticing the rack of women's golf attire hanging near where we are sitting. I am thinking, maybe with this increased sales success, I'll actually feel like I can afford to buy a smart-looking golf outfit like MaryAnn wears.

"Do you have any scripts for this?" I ask.

"There are no scripts. Through your sincere and careful listening and questioning, the clarity and the clearing comes naturally by following the buyer's lead. You will form each new question from the response that precedes it. Each answer that you receive brings the buyer closer to clarity."

"That is not the answer I wanted, but it sure makes a lot of sense. How do you suggest I begin implementing this tomorrow?"

"Continue with your focus on connection and now give the power to the customer. Your bottom line messages for your prospective clients with the Second C Principle are:

- *You know best what you and your company need.*
- *It's my job to assist you to make your best decision (even if it's not what I can provide).*

"This week, ask your prospects, 'What is most important and best for you?' "

"Mary Ann, that sounds way too simple. Without any script to memorize, I am nervous about coming up with good clarifying questions to ask!"

"I understand. At first, I was nervous about mastering the art of the 'Clarify' principle too. Then, after some trial and error, I learned to keep my attention on the client through my focused listening for what they were saying, instead of listening to my own inner nervous chatter about trying to do it right. Over time, I developed more trust in my ability to do that and it freed me up to be more present in the moment.

"Trust me. This simple, singular focus frees you up to be more present with the customer and relate more to their needs.

"Keep up the great work on your golf game and good luck on your sales appointments this week."

Chapter SEVEN

Monday

I've just come away from my first potential customer call this week. Woo Hoo! I did great with Connect and pretty good with my first shot at Clarify'. The customer was interested about our product and clear that it *is* what they want. I felt like he and I were working in partnership together—like a team focused on the same goal— integral in their product and their company decision. I enjoyed the feeling that I didn't need to control anything. I can't believe how easily I am changing my approach. And, I got more information about this company and their needs than I've ever received from a prospective customer on a first appointment.

However, when this potential customer said our product is a higher quality than they need, I didn't know how to help him clear that concern. I wanted to minimize, as I am so used to doing, but I knew that wouldn't work.

I wish I had explored further to discover if it was solely a pricing issue or if our product was not going to fit their needs at all. If it is a pricing issue, then I could determine if our company could create a product that would better fulfill their needs. Hopefully, I haven't blown this deal totally. I am going to call them back and see if I can continue the dialog.

Thursday

MaryAnn is a genius. She has given me the tools to rekindle the flame that I'd lost. I am playing a new game now. Those two new orders this week would have never happened with the old me. Helping customers gain clarity after building trust has changed the playing field. I don't have to coerce anybody to buy! And, they were happy when they made the decision to buy because their needs were being satisfied.

Now I understand what Charlie was telling me. The proposal I am preparing for this company could result in the largest sale I've ever made. I think it's time to call Charlie for that lunch date.

This second C Principle "Clarify" is such a respectful and honest way to deal with customers. I no longer feel the pressure to perform and make the sale. This is a much more genuine way to work with customers.

How can I make sure I am prepared for all these proposals I have scheduled for next week? I want to put my best foot forward and demonstrate my understanding of their needs, so I am offering them their best solution.

I'll give MaryAnn a call to see if I can take her to lunch tomorrow. I want her advice and to learn the third C Principle.

Chapter EIGHT

My luck! Mary Ann is available for lunch today. We agree to meet at a restaurant near Par's that's convenient for her, since she has to get back for a private lesson in the early afternoon. While we wait to be seated, I start sharing my news.

"MaryAnn, I am higher than a kite with news to share with you. I thought I almost blew it with a prospect this week, because I was at a loss as to how to help him get past a stumbling block. I followed up the next day and found that our product is too expensive because it has benefits they didn't need. So, I gained permission from the prospect to explore the possibility of providing a customized unit. And, guess what? My company said yes and he is placing an order."

The host seats us and brings water.

We raise our water glasses and drink a toast. I am so glad I picked a restaurant that's not noisy, and this booth gives us even more of a quiet space for conversation.

"Here is a toast to you, Dana, on your successes this week. Bravo!"

"Yes, but I'm concerned about my presentations this coming week. They mean a lot. I am counting on closing these sales."

"Dana, I understand how important those sales are for you. But, I'd like to share with you that it is not worth worrying about what will happen. It is about supporting your intention to do what's right for the customer. My mentor taught me the **I AM** equation: I + A = M, which stands for your *Intention* plus *Attention* equals *Manifestation* or the results you produce."

A young waitress hands us our menus and inquires about beverages. I set aside the menu, take out a small notebook and pen from my purse, and write down this I +A =M formula.

Intention (desire)

+

Attention (aligned actions)
Manifestation (result)

"Unlike a goal, which focuses on the result, a manifestation is the result of being clear on your *Intention* and putting your *Attention* on the Intention instead of the result. In other words, you make sure your language and actions are aligned with your Intention."

"So, let me see if I understand what you are saying. I need to let go of my attachment to making a sale and be open to all the different outcomes that are possible?"

"Yes, and," says MaryAnn, "understand that all those different possible outcomes are all also wins for all parties.

"It's a process of *Connecting* and *Clarifying* and lastly, *Cultivating.* The third C Principle is *"Cultivate."* This principle includes the element of

Intention which is to create the ultimate, mutually beneficial outcome. For example, a variety of outcomes are possible, and they are all in this relationship-based approach—all of which you must see are a win for everyone. For example, it could mean a sale for you of greater magnitude than you could imagine. It could mean you refer the client somewhere else that best serves their needs. It could mean you get referrals. You see? When you are committed to a mutual win, everyone wins."

The young waitress is back to take our order. We are so focused on our conversation that the interruption barely intrudes on our flow of conversation.

Mary Ann continues, "The trick is letting go of your attachment to needing the sale. Dana, think about a client contact you are going to make tomorrow. What is your Intention for that conversation?"

"Well, let's see. My Intention is to connect and begin to build trust."

"Good. So, what Attention will support you in fulfilling your Intention?"

"Oh, I am beginning to see what you are getting at. This helps me to focus on my Intention, doesn't it? The Attention that will support me is listening for what will best serve the client, using language that conveys my caring, asking questions that clarify her needs, and, well, basically everything I have been learning so far!"

"Yes, by keeping mindful of your 'I + A =M,' you will be more effective in producing satisfying results for you and your customer."

"So, MaryAnn, tell me more about *Cultivate.*"

In between bites of her chicken Caesar salad, she continues, "OK, the third C Principle, *Cultivate,* means bringing the exchange to a mutually beneficial conclusion and setting the stage for next steps. Simply put, help the client obtain what they want. Remember, though, whether you get the actual sale or not—either way—it is about cultivating a long term relationship of highest respect. In this way, you never lose a customer."

I jot a note in my notebook and reflect on what she just said as I chew a bite of my seafood salad. "Mr. Cummings won't understand if I don't make the sale. He is all about the bottom line. And, I need to pay the mortgage."

"Dana, two weeks ago I told you about the first C Principle, *Connect*. You tried it and you came back happy because of your ability to create relationships. Last week I gave you the second C Principle, *Clarify*. So far you have already achieved more satisfying results than you have been in the past few years. So, if you do nothing more, you are already much farther ahead than you were three weeks ago before we met. I am asking you to trust the process, and you will obtain greater results and feel better about yourself. Are you willing to try?"

"You haven't steered me wrong up to this point. I guess I am just worried about failing. Tell me more about *Cultivate*."

"OK, take out your notebook, and we will go over the key elements of the third C - Cultivate:

- Facilitate the client: what/when/how they will proceed
- Reinforce the value of the relationship
- Plant seeds for continuing the relationship
- Trust in the process/outcome (I + A = M)
- Acknowledge the client

"Wow! It sounds like I have a *lot* more to learn. I have no idea what most of this means. It all seems so foreign to me."

"Really, Dana, the bottom-line of *Cultivate* is about helping the client obtain what they want or need. Assisting the customer to move forward toward what they want—whatever that is and whatever it takes. As I said before, the key to this 3C Principle is holding your focus on the customer's needs instead of your own. Dana, have you ever sold something to someone that they didn't really want or need?"

"No. But, I have to be honest. I've tried many times. Hmmm, maybe that's one of the reasons I haven't been making as many sales."

The waitress clears our plates and inquires about coffee or dessert. We each order a cup of coffee, and then Mary Ann asks, "So, what is your game plan for this week?"

"Ok. I get your point. I'll give this a try. What do I have to lose? Alright then, tell me more about *Cultivate*. When I meet with my prospects this week to present my proposals, how do I close the sale?"

"From what you have experienced with me, and what you have learned so far about the 3C Principle, what do you think your strategy/approach should be?"

A former golf student recognizes Mary Ann and comes over to our table. She apologizes for the interruption and asks Mary Ann a question, which gives me some time to think.

Returning her attention to me, Mary Ann hasn't dropped the thread of our conversation. She asks me again, "What do you think your approach should be?"

"I guess if I believe that they know what's best for them, I have successfully facilitated their clarity, and I have presented options that are in their best interests, the decision, regardless of whether or not they buy from me, is a natural conclusion."

"Terrific, and there is more to *cultivating* than coming to a conclusion. Cultivating also includes supporting the customer in following through. For example, when you were clear that you were going to rent the clubs instead of purchase, and you wanted individual lessons with me, I asked you, 'What day would you like to schedule your first lesson?'

You are supporting your client in successfully following through. For example, you could invite them to take their next step, such as filling out the order blank, reviewing the contract, or filing out the purchase order form. You could schedule check-in dates for support and accountability."

"Yes, but what if my prospect decides they are happy with the products they are buying from my competitor? What do I do about that?"

"Appreciate that *that* is their best decision now, and that you would like to continue your relationship with them for any future needs they may have. Or, you could ask them if they are willing for you to check in on their future needs. It's OK to let go and leave the door open. The 3 C Principle is no assurance of making a sale, but it does increase your probability substantially."

"I'm sold. It seems like doing the right thing will pay off greater dividends in the long run. Right?"

"Right, and your 3C Principle *Cultivate* bottom-line message you want to leave with your client is this question, 'How can I continue to support your success?'

"Now, I think you are ready for your next big test. I've scheduled time for you and I to play nine holes on Saturday. Ready?"

Chapter NINE

"Hi, MaryAnn. I thought I'd drop by the store to let you know how things are going. Do you have a few minutes right now or shall I give you a call?"

"Hi Dana, yes, I have a few minutes right now. I look forward to hearing how it's going for you. And, by the way, that was a great round of golf last week. I know your golf game is improving. How did your proposal presentations go this week?"

"MaryAnn, on a scale of 1-10, this week was a 15! I have never felt so comfortable in making a sale without selling. Of the six presentations, four placed orders and one was quite sizeable; one I referred to someone else and, on the sixth one, we are still looking at additional options. What a strange feeling, referring business to someone else, but I know that it was the right thing for that client. And, most importantly, they know that I was doing what was best for them. So, I believe the door is open for a long term relationship.

"Mr. Cummings came into my office today and told me he was thrilled with my new sales and the new customers. I also had lunch with Charlie this week, thanked him profusely for being so honest with me, and shared with him my new outlook on how I am going to conduct my business from now on. I also apologized to Charlie for taking him for granted in the past. In fact, I have set up meetings with the majority of my customers to rebuild my connections with them.

"You know, I had certain reservations about this 'letting go,' but it feels natural and the right thing to do, rather than trying to sell something to someone who doesn't need it or want it."

A customer asks Mary Ann a question about lessons. I am aware I must not take up any more of her time right now.

"I am very proud of you for the courage it has taken to try the 3C Principle. It isn't easy to change old habits. It often takes adversity for people to recognize the need to change."

"Thank you. The company annual golf tournament is tomorrow. I'll call you and let you know how it went. I am certain that with your coaching, I'll have a good time. And do you know the best part, MaryAnn? I feel like I have you for a new friend, and I am considering buying golf clubs. Can you believe it?!"

"Well, I am glad you stopped by, because I have something for you."

MaryAnn waves for me to follow her down a hallway to her office. She goes over to her top desk drawer and pulls out a bright yellow laminated 5"x 7" card and hands it to me. It is a duplicate of the one her mentor had given her.

"Wow, MaryAnn, this is very thoughtful of you! Thanks."

And then she hands me a golf shirt with the Par's logo on it.

"Thanks, Mary Ann!

"You are very welcome. It has been a pleasure to share the 3C Principle with you and watch you apply those principles with such great success."

Chapter TEN

(Three months later)

"Brandon, I can't be late. It is the quarterly sales meeting today." Brandon is still eating his oatmeal breakfast.

"OK, Mom, I'm almost ready."

Breakfast on the run, as usual. I check myself in the hallway mirror on the way out the door. I'm wearing my red suit today with a white silk shell and my red pumps. For a fleeting moment, I debate about adding accessories, but I really don't have time to deal with it. Even though this suit is well-worn and it's seen better days, this is still my "power suit" because I feel more confident when I it. I'm told it goes really well with my blond hair. Speaking of my hair, I can't help but notice I am overdue for a haircut—getting a little shaggy around my neck.

Oh well, things are looking up.

In the car, on the way to his school, I take the opportunity to tell Brandon how much I have appreciated his patience and support as I have dealt with this crisis situation. He gives me a big smile and lets me hug him before he gathers up his backpack and escapes.

I rush to the office. I am excited about the meeting today, as I know my sales have increased dramatically over the last six months.

Mr. Cummings is already in the conference room and he is wearing a navy suit, white shirt, and a solid red tie. He is deflecting jibes from the sales reps about how unusually dressed up he is today. The other thing I notice is the smell of coffee and a faint whiff of chocolate, instead of the usual fragrance of maple bars. *What is going on here today?* That's when I see the sheet cake with chocolate icing next to the coffee pot on the back table. *This is unusual!*

Mr. Cummings unceremoniously starts the meeting, reviews overall company results, and proceeds to announce sales awards the same way he always does. Here is the usual round of polite applause. Nothing different about that!

Except for the fact that sales awards have been handed out, yet he hasn't called my name. What is happening? I know that I have improved. My excitement has now turned to anxiety.

"Today we would like to give special recognition to a member of our team who has doubled her sales volume and set a new record for highest sales volume in a quarter. This person has a renewed energy and enthusiasm, and she has brought in many of our most satisfied new customers in the last six months. It is with absolute pleasure that I present this special award to Dana Sullivan."

Amid the spontaneous applause and attagirls, I stand and take a bow. Wow! All those things he said about me. I am thrilled to know that my hard work and willingness to change has brought the kind of success I haven't experienced in years! I can't wait to tell Carol and Mary Ann.

"Thank you, Mr. Cummings. It's an honor to be a part of the Innovative Products team."

Mr. Cummings directs our attention to the cake and coffee in the back of the room. I take time to socialize with my colleagues, as I join the others for coffee and chocolate cake.

On my way out of the meeting, a young sales rep named William asks, "How did you achieve that tremendous increase in sales? My sales are slacking, and I could really use some advice." He seems quite young, and I know he is new to the company. I have empathy for what he must be feeling.

"William, my secret is this, I stopped selling. Are you willing to change some or all of your habits in order to achieve greater success?"

"Most definitely, if you will help me."

"It would be my pleasure, William. Let's head down to my office, and I will share what I have learned."

Over another cup of coffee, I pull out the bright yellow laminated reminder card that Mary Ann gave me. I keep it handy in my purse because I refer to it several times a day. I told William about my teacher and new friend, Mary Ann, and then I shared all about my new success formula, the 3Cs.

Epilogue

Six months later:

Dana and MaryAnn continued to build their friendship.

Dana bought a set of new golf clubs, shoes, and two golf outfits. She now plays golf several times a week and has made new friends on the golf course.

William increased his sales and continues to hone his skills.

Innovative Products continued to expand their customizing capabilities, based on customer input and demand.

Dana spends more quality time with Brandon, and they are now playing golf together at least one weekend a month.

Epilogue

One year later:

Due to Dana's sustained success and William's growing success, Mr. Cummings offered Dana a promotion to Director of Sales and Training.

Dana didn't want to manage sales people, so she negotiated the position of Director of Training, so she could mentor members of the sales team in the 3C Principle approach, while continuing to cultivate her existing customer relationships.

She enjoys the security that her new financial income affords, and she appreciates being able to continue to do what she enjoys most: helping empower others to fulfill their needs.

The 3C Principle

Connect

"What is the one thing I can help you with today?"

- Be service oriented versus sales focused
- Be caring and fully present; LISTEN deeply
- Be considerate of the client's agenda, not mine
- Be a collaborative partner
- Be committed to the quality of the relationship

Clarify

"What is most important and best for you?"

- Support the client in identifying what is best for them
- Assist the client is clearing the barriers to what they need
- Explore options and generate possibilities
- Empower the client's decision-making process
- Acknowledge and respect their choices

Cultivate

"How can I continue to support your success?"

- Facilitate the client: what/when/how they will proceed
- Reinforce the value of the relationship
- Plant seeds for continuing the relationship
- Trust in the process/outcome (I + A = M)
- Acknowledge the client

The 3C Principle

Connect   (*What is the one thing I can help you with today?*)

- Be service oriented versus sales focused

- Be caring and fully present; LISTEN deeply

- Be considerate of the client's agenda, not mine

- Be a collaborative partner

- Be committed to the quality of the relationship

Clarify   (*What is most important and best for you?*)

- Support the client in identifying what is best for them

- Assist the client is clearing the barriers to what they need

- Explore options and generate possibilities

- Empower the client's decision-making process

- Acknowledge and respect their choices

Cultivate   (*How can I continue to support your success?*)

- Facilitate the client: what/when/how they will proceed

- Reinforce the value of the relationship

- Plant seeds for continuing the relationship

- Trust in the process/outcome (I + A = M)

- Acknowledge the client

Authors' Reflections

Mark Bornstein

Our short story conveys the principles of coaching as a means to improve interpersonal skills with clients, friends, and family. As we examine the traditional sales model, it is based on meeting quotas and selling product. With the changes in technology and the instant information available on the Internet, the role of the salesperson has changed to that of a facilitator who can become an integral part of the decision-making process. Dana is very typical of the salesperson of old and throughout our story Mary Ann has inspired and coached her on the facilitation process that we have called *The 3C Principle*.

As a salesperson for over 40 years, I met my co-author who was President of the Academy for Coach Training, and I spent two years becoming a Certified Professional Coach. *I was Dana.* The paradigm shifted in my mind as I learned how to be a facilitator (coach) to my clients. I learned that these coaching principles can be applied to all areas of my life—not just sales. It has made a major difference in how I communicate and am present with family, friends, and associates.

Being a college professor early in my career, I have been an avid reader of sales books and books on cultural and interpersonal experiences. All of these books offered something to be gleaned. I have tried and experimented with so many sales theories yet NEVER before have I seen the success that I have enjoyed since learning this facilitation model of the *3C Principle.*

Does this mean that you need to go to coaching school to learn how to sell more effectively? No, but you can learn the lessons that I learned and that our character Dana learned.

In learning these principles, I have experienced more fun in my role as a sales facilitator—or maybe we should say "coaching partner" for "WIN – WIN" relationships.

This book came out of a conversation with Fran, sharing how the coaching model has changed my approach as a sales executive and trainer. This book is a collaborative process that started with an idea that was developed and worked on over several years. We hope we have caused you to examine yourself, how you sell, and how you treat and interact with your clients.

Fran Fisher

"Why me?" I asked Mark, when he invited me to co-author a book with him.

I knew Mark as a successful real estate broker and student enrolled in my coaching school. I learned that as a long-time real estate sales trainer, Mark was disheartened with the old sales paradigm and that as a student of coaching, he was inspired with a solution that would transform the definition for sales. Mark was clear that the coaching approach was the answer.

He convinced me that we would make a great team, each bringing our expertise for this storytelling venture.

I was inspired with the possibility of making a difference by providing this simple yet transformational mindset and skillset that is so transferrable in all our relationships. I've heard it said that "every conversation has inherent in it an element of 'sales.'" I have come to believe that is true. The 3C Principle provides a simple structure that, when applied, can have profound impact on the quality of your life and work. Try it!

 **Mark J. Bornstein,** MIRM, CPC is the president of The Bornstein Group and Vice President of The Force Realty. The Bornstein Group is a consulting firm that specializes in sales training, business consulting, and business and executive coaching. Mark's first book, *Energizing Your Sales,* focused on the basic fundamentals of new home sales.

Mark is a licensed real estate broker, educator, and consultant and has held executive positions with homebuilding companies in California and Washington. Mark holds the CSP, CMP, and MIRM designations and is a principal instructor for the IRM and CSP curriculum. Mark has been a featured guest speaker and has written articles for NAHB, SMI, and local associations. Committed to education, Mark owns a proprietary real estate school offering training and continuing education classes.

Mark holds the CPC coaching designation as he expanded his practice as a life and business coach. He works with individuals and companies to align values and empower the client, leading to greater productivity, balance, and happiness. This provides Mark with a toolbox of skills to help empower and improve the performance of salespeople and their organizations.

Mark lives with his wife in Redmond, Washington, and has two grown children.

The Bornstein Group Inc.
Web Site: www.thebornsteingroup.com
Email: mjb2049@gmail.com
Phone: 425.444.2084
Your partner for success

 **Fran Fisher**, Master Certified Coach (MCC) Your Vision=My Passion!

Fran is a visionary leader, international speaker, and published author. She specializes in working with entrepreneurs, executives, and collaborative teams providing coaching services including the Living Systems Approach® to Collaborative Work Groups, Living Your Vision®, Dependable Strengths, Learning in Action EQ Assessment, and Core Values Index.

Recognized internationally as one of the pioneers and champions for coaching, Fran served as a founding board member of the International Coach Federation (ICF), chair of the Credentialing Program Committee for aspiring coaches and coach training schools, and she was the first Executive Director of the Association for Coach Training Organizations (ACTO). Currently, Fran specializes in mentoring coaches at all levels.

Fran is founder of the Living Your Vision® (LYV) transformational process, and the Academy for Coach Training (ACT), one of the first three coaching schools accredited by ICF. In 2005, Fran sold the LYV and ACT businesses to inviteCHANGE, located in Edmonds, Washington, USA.

Fran enjoys empowering her clients to improve their performance, profitability, and personal fulfillment, and she helps them close the gap between their highest visions and their current reality.

Fran Fisher is the author of *Violet's Vision,* and a contributing author to several collections including *Chocolate for a Woman's Soul,* and *NO Winner Ever Got There Without A Coach.* She lives in Bellevue, Washington, USA.

FJFisher Coaching and Consulting
Web Site: www.franfishercoach.com
Email: fran@franfishercoach.com
Phone: 425.401.1374

Please feel free to inquire regarding further services available:

Fran Fisher

One-on-one coaching

Living Your Vision®

Mentoring for coaches

The 3C Principle workshops and teleclasses

Mark Bornstein

Sales training and coaching

Web Site: www.empowermentselling.com